Life, Death and Somethings Inbetween

Ulrica Cooper

First published in 2025 by Paragon Publishing, Rothersthorpe
© Ulrica Cooper 2025

The rights of Ulrica Cooper to be identified as the author of this work have
been asserted by her in accordance with the Copyright. Designs and Patents
Act of 1988.

ISBN 978-1-78792-095-8

Book design, layout and production management by Into Print
www.intoprint.net
+44 (0)1604 832149

CONTENTS

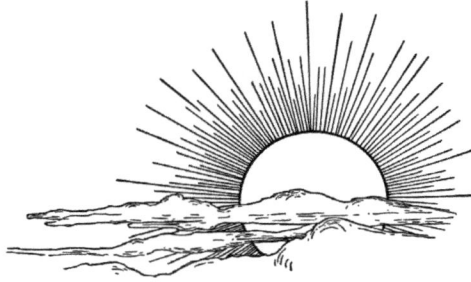

I would like to dedicate this book to anyone who has sunk to the deep, dark bottom of the ocean and then found their way, somehow, back to the surface and sunlight.

Also, I hope that my poems give hope to those still struggling in the murky depths by helping them believe that there is a way through. Spiritual healing, especially learning to forgive, has saved my sanity and probably my life.

PURPOSE

To see beyond the decaying flesh,
To notice the warmth shining through the cold, white skin,
To remember the laughter and soft embraces
While all around lie dreams shattered on the sick bed.

To known and keep the knowledge that love never dies,
To see them dancing on warm sands of the eternal beach,
To hold within my heart the tender rose petals
That will never fade nor shrivel.

I believe this is my purpose
To see beyond the misery and death
To look beyond this illusionary world
And know that eternal love radiates through the veils of hate.

To love my brother despite his crimes,
To bathe his wounds and keep them clean,
To stretch out my hand to aid his climb
Knowing that while I hold his hand, he also holds mine.

WINTER

Aah the beauty of winter, and yet so harsh,
The apricot blush of sunset, soft and low,
Enhancing silhouettes of interlaced branches.
How we love the perfect, sparkling, pristine snow
But hate the frost-bitten fingers of those without a home,
Without a blanket and nowhere to go.

Snowball-fighting children, run and play,
Shrieks of laughter and delight,
Running to mother to warm their hands,
Some have their mothers in the cold of night,
Others call out to the fathomless sky, piercing blue,
'Help!' mocks the echo from the hill of white.

Radiant Venus, hanging so brightly,
Like a Christmas bauble on the tree,
Watches families stuff their faces with turkey,
Sweet puddings and whatever else they see.
In the snowy forest the little deer stumbles,
Whilst looking for food, she falls on her knee.

Softly, snowflakes freckle her face,
Mother deer nudges her, 'Stand up child.
The snow is deep, the forest a glistening diamond
But the wolves are out, running and wild!'
Nurtured children will be tucked up in bed,
Protected by parental love, kind and mild.

GRIEF

Those lips to kiss
Our hearts entwine
I am his
And he is mine.

But where, Oh where
Is he now?
The stabbed heart
The perplexed brow.

I search the town
I search my heart
How deep the pain
Now we're apart.

And yet in dreams
He calls my name
He declares his Love
I do the same.

Our souls unite.
Were they ever split?
He was always there
Just not aware of it.

OUR CONNECTION

Everyone touches our hearts,
In one form or another,
A secret whisper or a loud shout,
From a sister, friend or lover.
Or even by an opponent,
A catalyst or avenger.
Each tiny nudge or sentence,
Keeps us safe or in danger.

No man is an island,
Or so the saying goes,
Each breathe we exhale,
Is someone else's clothes.
Each strand of hair we lose,
Each flake of skin we shed,
Will create another's carpet,
Will blanket someone's bed.

We cannot live in isolation
For even thoughts impact,
Upon other minds and hearts,
Always keeping close contact.
Try to be open and aware
Of the flowers that you send,
Be them sweet and lovely
Or with thorns to tear and rend.

70 YEARS CELEBRATION OF THE NHS

1948 was the year it started,
Aneurin Bevan was the man at the wheel,
"Cure them all!" This Minister imparted,
"Build better hospitals and they'll surely heal."
"Young, old, rich, poor, black, brown or white,
Free healthcare will soon end their plight!"

A seed of an idea took hold in a compassionate man,
All of seventy years ago,
The seed grew and the N.H.S. began,
Britain would put an end to misery and woe,
Bedpans, bandages, syringes and medication
Were now available to the whole Nation.

Numerous nurses and doctors were promptly recruited,
Then came the therapists and admin too,
Cleaners, porters, caterers and laundry folk all contributed,
Everyone grafted hard, there was always so much to do.
Hold a hand, transfuse some blood, and operate
with anaesthetic,
Assist a patient to walk, enable them to talk, be patient
and sympathetic.

Now, and for years, the service is struggling to make ends meet,
More patients to attend and more demands are being made,
The staff, their duties they are juggling,
"Please let me rest my feet."
Cutting back on employees and the amount that they're paid,
This amazing idea has more problems than enough,
But the essence that drives it is the belief in Love.

This suffering, this human tragedy unearthed a love so deep,
a kindness so beautiful.
Did he sacrifice himself to help us delve into these realms,
to bring us closer together?
To discover this bounty in our souls?

THE STAR

The star is bright, worshipped, adored.
Flocks follow and surround him,
The press praises and elevates him,
Luxurious presents abound him,
National attention elates him.

What would happen if the audience turns its back?
Would he still believe he's real?
Still shimmer without their glare?
His own self-love could he feel?
Or nakedly chill as if stripped bare?

A ROSE

There was a beautiful rose
That grew by a high wall,
Not everyone could see it
Because it wasn't very tall,
Then one day a gale arrived
And blew down the wall with glee,
Now the loveliness of the rose
Was there for all to see.

STILL HERE

You can't see me but I am still here,
You can't hear me yet I am very near,
My love is in the sunset and sunrise,
My tears are in the hellos and goodbyes,
My voice is the flutter of leaves on trees,
My face is in flowers nourishing bees,
There is no death of love and affection,
Its smile shimmers eternally in your direction.

BLOSSOMS

Out come the blossoms as soft as snow,
How long they will last no-one will know,
They bring the promise of youthful spring,
When hearts and feet will dance and sing.

DENIAL

Blinder than bats,
Heads more buried than ostrich's.
Is any creature more in denial
Than a human?

Fly and drive everywhere,
Release filth into the air,
Why worry?
We only need to breathe it in.

"Why stop our fun?
The world's our playground,
We are the important ones here,
Sorry, forgot about our kids!"

FREEDOM

Oh this body, this armour, this restraint!
Let me fly over the trees,
The houses, the land,
Flap my wings, soaring!

My love, my energy flows
And pushes to expand
To embrace all living things.
Let me touch the Moon
And dance around the stars.

I wish to swim an ocean
And paint a million portraits.
Let me sing, and run and race,
And fill the world with the expanse of my being,
Let me free of this mortal coil!

THE MOON IS STILL THERE

The shops are bare,
The cops say 'Don't you dare
Go out and socialise! '
But the Moon is still there.

Self isolate, don't congregate,
Cooped up like poor chickens
For Sunday roasts
But the Moon is still there.

The world is on its head,
Safest place is my bed,
Wear a mask, over-wash your hands,
And the Moon is still there.

Fears crashing in,
Order thoughts, where to begin?
The unknown is becoming known,
Aah but the Moon is still there!

Waiting, Quiet, Cleaner air,
Cars resting,
Food digesting at a slower pace,
And the Moon is still there.

Let me out! Let me free, let go of me!
I can do what I WISH,
Stop controlling me!
And yet, the Moon is still there.

Don't shake hands, in fact 'Don't touch',
Don't even look my way,
It's all too much,
But even so, the Moon is still there.

A surreal dream?
A different planet?
The world is topsy-turvey and I'm still on it,
Thank goodness that the Moon is still there.

HOLLY TREE

What a microscopic, prickly world,
Entwining and confusing branches,
Tweet, tweet, chirrup, chirrup,
Fluttering tiny wings.

Branch hopping Blackbird,
Sings from tree's crown,
What insects reside here?
How many nestling chicks?

Melding shape congregations,
With flurries of rainbows,
A cacophony of twittering, cooing and calling,
A secret world where I cannot enter.

Only a fairy could fit,
I'll admire from the outside,
Let the merry-go-round be safe,
This tree, carefully, holds her family in her prickly arms.

YOUTH

Free as a bird,
Out in the blue,
Kissed by the sun,
Loving the view.

Head full of dreams,
Inspired by the calm,
Irrepresible youth,
Nature's the balm.

The world is her oyster,
Where will she go?
Dancing her dance,
Reaching high, falling low.

The bounce of youth
Will keep her afloat,
Zig-zagging through life,
Steering her boat.

2020

This is the year that sank like a ship,
The dreaded C had us in its grip.
Plastic gloves and plastic gown,
Visors, masks, I felt like a clown.

A new year is dawning pretty soon,
Hope is fawning, rising like the moon.
Closer than ever, our strength has flourished,
Freedom laced with love will keep us nourished.

MY LIFE

I made a decision
Eons ago,
That much of my life
Would be filled with woe.
Before this incarnation I chose to see,
If I could become a better me.

My mother's rejections
Sliced like a knife,
She chose an escape, instead of life.
My father's violence pulled me down,
My anger grew,
It fit like a crown.

The fury in my cells
Has torn me into shreds,
Keeping me away
From loved ones beds.
I will keep forgiving
To let go of this pain,
I will find peace
And live fully again!

SUMMER

I have never heard a bird sing a sad song,
A spring is in their step, they know they belong,
They confidently strut and fly with ease and grace,
Their soft, firm feathery bodies the Sun will embrace.

We cherish Nature together, enraptured by the peace,
This vivacious bounty is thriving, and will never cease.
Bright coloured, and soft pastel, blossoms delight,
Dancing leaves are laughing, bleached by the light.

Now evening's golden light tenderly enfolds my skin,
I feel cherished and swaddled, night will soon begin.
My feathered friends take their leave, fluttering to their nest,
Leaving me in the balmy twilight, relaxed and needing rest.

WINTER

Softly, spiraling, silent snow,
Swirling blobs of snowflakes.
A frozen, gentle hush decends,
Heaven, how my heart aches.

To be immersed in mystery
Other-wordly magic peace
A twinkling blanket everywhere,
A pristine pearly fleece.

THE SACRED SONG

"Remember? Do you?"
"What?"
"TRY, try to remember",
"What? Space? Stars? Planets
Orbiting through the dark?
Connecting in the expanse?
Pulsating, reaching, touching.
Star explosions? Starlight!?"

"The Sacred Song,
The Sacred Sound,
Hidden deep
Within your Soul."

"Pounding, vibrating,
Embracing me in my fears,
Comforting, rocking my baby.
Soothing away my tears.
Remember the sweet moments;
Grey rabbits hopping at dusk,
Mum's soft hand as we follow
The field's curving path.

Warm feelings, tender thoughts inside:
Family gatherings before he died,
Our ginger kitten's innocent face,
Watch it darting all over the place.
Kiss its soft and fluffy fur
The Sacred Song dwells there.

Vague images of a break up,
Tears spilling from my heart.
Desolation, loneliness,
Believing Love and I are apart.
When healing my pain through a prayer
The Sacred Song lives there."

MOTHER EARTH

She is our Mother, a loving Mother
Albeit, sometimes, a dangerous one.
Each tiny berry and seed is her precious gift,
Her profound, luscious forests in various greens,
Whispering seas of corn, wheat and barley
Are whipped or caressed by her breath.
Beasts, beetles, butterflies and bees
Are all her beloved pets
Not forgetting the reptiles, birds and fish,
Any crawling, flying, swimming thing.

How generous she is, and yet she also takes away,
With voluminous floods and terrifying earthquakes,
And ferocious, scarlet, sulphurous volcanic spit.
Battering us and all other life forms.
But these wounds hurt her too.
They crack her skin and scar her soils.
Must we add to these afflictions?
Should we poison her waters?
Choke and blacken her breath?
Should we blindfold our eyes or open them wide?
Cherish our Mother as she nourishes and cherishes us?

PHOENIX STRUGGLES

There is a Phoenix inside of me,
Desperate to burst out,
For me to be reborn.
Yet my past grasps its heels,
Digs in its nails,
Whispers in its ears.

"Don't forget she's selfish!"
"He tore your heart out!"
"Don't trust! Keep them away!
Isolate yourself for another day."
Pulled in opposite directions,
"Free yourself!" "Let it go!"

I can't, I can, I will, I won't,
Need to drop my shackles,
Flap my Phoenix wings,
Ascend from the blaze.
Let my destructive flesh melt
And burn to grey ashes.

A new, robust, healthy skin
Forms around my bones.
My soul is growing,
Surviving and thriving.
Now my Phoenix
Is roosting on the roof tops.
Surveying the World from above.

THE MIRROR

Who takes from you?
Who hates your colour?
Who despises your sex?
Knocks you down?
Leaves you out?
Who sneers at your clothes?
Belittles your music choices?
Why do you feel on the outside?
That no-one approves of you,
Neither loves nor wants you?

Who is this Other?
There is no Other,
Only mirrors, reflecting
Wounds we need to heal.
We are all connected.
All one with the Great, Loving Source.

Forgive yourself and you will forgive others,
Free yourself and you will, definately,
Free others.
Who is this other?
Only an aspect of yourself.

A FURRY FRIEND

Scuffling and scrambling
In heaped dead leaves,
Nose – twitching – and an electric tail,
Sharp, bright, searching eyes,
So quick, he takes me by surprise.

Furry, brown body darting
Between low lying plants,
Scratching for food,
Racing the clock to avoid danger.
I love the presence of this tiny stranger.

Women shriek at the sight,
Men throw heavy things his way,
Traps are set indoors
Tools of extermination they employ
But for me, he brings perfect joy.

TRANSCENDENCE

I am lost,
Foundation-less,
Floating, drifting.
Transcending?

Where do I go from here?
Step on a cloud,
Is it safe?
Can it hold my weight?

Am I to be cradled?
Swaddled in soft arms?
Soft but strong,
Supporting and loving?

I have left the jetty,
Am jumping through the air,
Look for a rainbow,
Cross my fingers and TRUST !

HI ROBIN

When full of despair and dismay,
Night enshrouding my day,
Blood pumping in my ears,
Nothing to allay my fears,
Yet, if I hear your shrill,
Beautiful song,
Oh sweet robin your tunes
Help me along!

As light and sprightly as can be,
English emblem we can agree,
Through wars and germs you still thrive,
Let our nation unite to keep you alive.
Cultivate hedges and trees,
Repair the soil please!
Our Christmas card bird is a beauty,
Looking after it is our duty.

Delicate but strong
Keep on with your cheeps,
We cherish your presence,
We love you for keeps.

LONELINESS

The little girl inside of me is here,
She's waiting, always waiting...
For the day that she becomes a woman,
For the day when she feels secure,
For the night she can spend in her lover's arms,
Knowing...
that she is loved and wanted.

The hours are always long,
The silence very deep,
Except for the voices of anxiety,
Nagging in her head.

I don't want to see her
Or to say, "Hello",
She always looks too vulnerable to me.

DRINKING THEIR LIVES AWAY

Tattered baggies hanging loose,
Cool and clear sunny dawn,
Homing benches, broken glass,
Wrinkled faces, life forlorn.

Fermented liquid stale and strong,
Trickles down his greedy throat,
It's never enough, "Never enough!"
Passers-by observe and gloat.

Watch them tripping, watch them laughing,
Through their rotting teeth,
Lazy sunbathing browns their faces,
Stagnant odours rise from underneath.

Self medication is the answer,
Don't underestimate its attraction,
Obliterate another daytime,
Yearning love but settling for distraction.

LOST AND FOUND

"It's time to feather the nest," he said.
Our baby bird fell out long ago."
It flapped its tiny, new-grown feathers
But could not lift up from the ground.

Its parents searched but could not find,
Full of anger, angst and woe,
"Stupid baby! Where has it gone?
Why could he not wait for us?"
Baby bird floundered, faltered and reeled,
In confusion and dread on the forest floor,
Mother bird scanned the wood,
And waited patiently for his return.

The nest became brittle and mouldy,
Old moss and twigs fell into the abyss,
The parents, also, lost some feathers
In their state of dismay and worry.

One day father bird brought fresh moss,
Mother collected young leaves and twigs,
"Let's make a nest anew to prepare
For when he returns to us."

After many lucky escapes,
Baby bird's feathers had grown.
He had become stronger
On sleepy insects.

Up he fluttered from one small branch
To the next, chirping,
Until he finally reached his parents
And the newly feathered nest.

THE UNDERGROUND STORY

Mr. Garden Gnome in his green suit,
White beard and red cap,
Stands next to a plastic toadstool,
The red and white, poisonous kind.

He's standing on a brick
And his beady eyes
Can see many sacred things
Hidden in the grass and earth.

Families of ants scuttle and ferry food
From one place to the next.
Hover flies dance from flower to flower,
Hoping birds will mistake them for a wasp.

The earth is dry, light brown and crumbly.
After rain the slugs, snails and worms
Creep out from their deep, damp
Subterranean sanctuaries.

A few pretty, petite daisies
Seek out the sun to refresh their faces.
Under early, fallen leaves hides
A coiled, sleeping centipede.

Birds waddle past looking for food,
Beetles, bugs run for cover
Under stones and foliage,
Some just aren't quick enough.

Orange and scarlet berries
Have been released to the floor,
A robin and wood pigeons
Delicately feast on them.

I'm sure Mr Gnome has, also, seen
Numerous rats and mice,
Who crept out in the dusk
To play and scavenge in the Moonlight.

LEMURIA

Lemuria, O Lemuria,
Where did you go?
Under the waves,
Vanished without a trace in the flow?
An ancient civilisation,
Advanced beyond our dreams,
Sensitive and loving,
At one with crags and streams.

Visitors from many light years away,
Guided here by sunlight,
Came to explore but decided to stay.
You compassionately
And carefully tended our Earth,
A gentler World was imagined
And with toil was given birth.
Friends with the animals,
Ever deeply cherished.
Respected and nurtured,
This relationship was established.
Secrets captured in crystals,
Concealed in dark, damp caves,
Swept away forever, with it all,
In the tragic Sunami waves.

CHRISTMAS SPIRIT

Christmas warmth, Christmas light,
Christmas love holds me tight.
Forget the Holly, forget the baubles.
Forgive your enemy and their foibles,

Sing "Away In A Manger",
Bring kindness to a stranger,
Feed the cold and hungry now,
Include them in your Christmas vow.

Stop buying junk to fill the bins,
Pour away whisky, wines and gins,
The real spirit of Christmas is given with grace.
Smile, reach out, welcome and embrace.

Search the alleyways and pubs,
Search the streets and the clubs,
Entice the lonely away from their lair,
Bring love and laughter to ease their despair.

LITTLE BIRD

Somehow, I knew you'd come here,
As if from nowhere you appeared,
Your bright, proud, fluffy breast
But oh so tiny!
Held up by stick legs.

You sang to me as I topped up your seeds,
Perfectly balanced on a holly branch,
How wonderfully beautiful you are,
In a fragile flutter you are gone.

HUSH

I know a secret that no-one else knows,
If you hush you will know it too.
Beyong the rattling traffic,
Beyond the stiffling, polluted air,
Above the glorious, ma jestic trees
And the malignant skyscrapers,
Towards the stars, yet above them.
A place of love and wisdom,
A place of peace where I can rest my head,
Where dreams undreamed reveal
Their mysterious worlds, the resting place
For beautiful thoughts and prayers,
And eternal, blissful consciousness.

SEARCHING FOR PEACE

Watching waddling wood pigeons,
Peck, peck their bird food,
Helps me breathe, relax,
Soak in nature's green energy.
Trying to clear my mind and heart,
Images of their last breath.
Wheeled in and wheeled out,
I'm shocked by the speed of it all.
Thankfully, they usually slept deep
Before they fell into eternal slumber,
Numbed by pain killers
To aid this inevitable exit.

Trying to keep calm and composed,
Dr's panicky eyes challenge me,
"What to do? What to do?"
"Where to start? "What's the answer?"
Shortage of nurses, "They're off sick!"
Forget my job description,
Just gently wash and change their
Tired, hot, aching bodies.
Make them comfortable.

Bre e eath, hell I need a hug!
Not allowed! Need to cry, to grieve
But have to stand strong.
Feed the birds; grieve now,
Watch their soft bodies
And their ducking heads.
Obliviously, being sated.

They save my sanity,
Like colleagues, now friends,
Dearer than life itself!
Working together, holding on
And holding up as one.
Unbelievably, two years on,
A light shone, far end of the tunnel.
Crawling through each day,
Praying for that rainbow.

Searching for former normality.
A glimmer, a blue sky!
"Goodbye treacherous bug!"
"WELCOME BACK MY PLACID LIFE."

UNCONDITIONAL LOVE

I love you because you are free,
Because you don't actually need me.
Adorned with prickles, or short mouse hair,
Whiskered and fluffy, or scaled and bare.
Croaking, squatting, jumping into ponds,
Iridescent wings resting on fern fronds,
Wriggling, jiggling, hundreds of legs,
Fluttering, clucking and laying eggs.
Found in a flock, drove or a pride,
Under a cruel hot Sun or up midnight trees to hide,
Feasting on berries, ants, shoots or reeds,
Diving for fish; fulfilling offspring's needs.
I love you because you are free,
You aren't even aware of me,
I can't touch or cuddle you,
You just do what you need to do.

SOFTLY IS THE NIGHT

I love night time,
It can be lusciously soft,
Softly, dark blue,
Corners softened by shadows.

Softly padding paws of a fox,
Announced by the crash and tumble,
When he jumps and pulls over the bin,
Its contents sprawling over the floor.

Softly tiptoes the tiny feet of mice,
Scuttling into the food scraps,
Moving silently home,
Carrying pieces in their mouths.

Softly moves the creamy moon,
Laughing gently,
At the heads asleep,
On soft beds and pillows.

Strangers softly stumble,
In the dark, searching for light,
Seeking Love, home,
Peace and soft embraces.

THE GLASS

Half full, half empty, which is it?
Water – precious water,
Life sustainer, thirst quencher,
Swirling lakes, pelting rain,
Salty oceans.
Could contain alcohol,
Gulping throats, greedy appetites,
Bury painful emotions,
Laugh through tipsy tears.
Quaff strange potions.
Now empty; cracked lips,
Drought, unbearable thirst,
Weak with dehydration,
Crawl to seek an oasis.
Desperately in motion.
Search in the far off sands,
Where the glass was born.
Then furnaced and blown
In our homeland factories,
And handled with caution.

POPPY FIELDS

Their ghosts traipsed through poppies
Growing in far off fields,
Searching for their bleeding hearts
To be nurtured and be healed.

War blasted their security,
Their purpose and ambition.
Tore at their humanity
Without a hint of contrition.

Damaged and staggering
They tried to love from a place of pain,
Kindness shone through at times
But inconsistent again and again.

Blindly searching through the debris,
Trying this and trying that.
Grasping hope around its neck
Somehow believing the world is flat.

The signposts were distorted
And pointed the wrong way.
They carried on into the mire
Trudging through mud and clay.

They missed the Holy opening
The blessings and the light,
Fell increasingly into darkness,
A world consumed by night.

But suddenly in fields of poppies
And gorgeous cornflowers blue,
The Eternal Love comes fluttering
And Peace provides the view.

THE OLD FOX AND THE PUSSYCAT

Zigzagging, desperately hungry, old fox
Espied a black and white pussycat nearby.
She stopped in her tracks as he turned to say,
"We are meant to be enemies you and I".

The black and white feline replied,
"If it was morning I'd spit in your eye."
Shabby, pale coated fox agreed,
"I'd chase you through gardens in front of a passerby."
"I'd scratch your nose at noon
If you chased my mouse."
"And I'd bite your nose at teatime
If a human came out of their house."
But they agreed, "As it's sleep-time,
Everyone oblivious in bed,
We can be friends now
And just chat instead."

They sat in the garden
With the glorious moon in view,
Enjoying their secret
And happy rendezvous.

PIRATE TIME-SLIP

Would you believe it?
There's a Pirate in our midst?
Striding from a dark, dank alley
With rum on his breath,
A crooked, toothy smile
And skulduggery in his eyes.
2024, yet he struts his stuff fearlessly,
He knows 'The Swallow' is waiting
And a mast is an easy climb.
Straight from the portrait
That hangs on a tavern wall.
Adorned in a flowing, red silken jacket,
 Booted in knee high leather,
Brandishing a long, wooden walking stick.
A gold trimmed, three cornered hat
Hides his dark, greasy locks.
An embroidered waistcoat decorates his chest,
He proudly wears breeches for trousers,
Captain Hook would've proud to sup with him,
He'd have welcomed him onto his ship.

This enigma is lost in this twenty-first century,
He's taken a wrong turn through time.
He rides on a bus to the Thames,
Espies his galley ship with his telescope,
Scrambles up the rope ladder
And he and his mighty ship
Vanish in the river's mist.

FOR JAMES' BIRTHDAY

An azure sky, a warming sun,
Time to relax, the work is done,
Enjoy the peace, soak up the blue,
Hope all good things will come to you.

Also by Ulrica Cooper

A GREAT IDEA

A gentle children's story in which siblings, Mary and Tony, decide to build a rocket and fly to the Moon. While there, they meet a friendly Moon creature who wishes to return to Earth with them.
Back on Earth, this mysterious creature has the ability to talk to animals and fairies and, by doing so, helps the children to realise that all animals have their own beauty and purpose in Nature.

A Natural Beautiful You
Series

Creating Your Own Body Scrub

MONIQUE JOINER SIEDLAK

Oshun
Publications

Cover Design by MJS

Cover Image by dungthuyvunguyen@pixabay.com

Published by Oshun Publications

www.oshunpublications.com